Praise For
The Emotionally Abusive Parent

Anne has written a thoughtful, practical, and biblical book on a difficult topic. Her compassion for the sufferer is evident, and her use of the Scriptures brings comfort to the troubled heart. This book will be helpful to those who have suffered at the hands of an abusive parent and those who desire to help them.

Julie Ganschow, PhD.

Anne tackles a very difficult issue with compassion and skill. She helps us understand, through the lenses of Scripture, the lingering effects and current impact of parental mistreatment on adults. She offers biblical help and hope for those who believe that their past will keep them from living a fruitful life in the present.

Lou Priolo, PhD.

With years of counseling experience, Dr. Dryburgh is able to compassionately lay out potential sequelae of parental oppression in a concise and organized manner. Consistently she refers to Scripture and even more, to the true and living God of Scripture, for hope and healing.

Jenn Chen, PsyD, MABC, MA (MFT)

Anne Dryburgh has provided us with yet another helpful tool when dealing with abuse. In her book, The Emotionally Abusive Parent, she gives hope with clear steps for change and healing when children are verbally abused by one or both parents. As with all of Anne's books, she points to Christ as the sufficient one to heal and to give hope! She is quickly becoming the Christian voice for abuse victims. I wholeheartedly recommend all of her books.

Johnny Touchet, Pastor and Biblical Counselor

The Emotionally Abusive Parent

Also by Anne Dryburgh

*Debilitated and Diminished: Help for Christian Women
in Emotionally Abusive Marriages*

*(Un)ashamed: Christ's Transforming
Hope for Rape Victims*

*For 2022:
The Emotionally Abusive Husband
The Emotionally Abusive Mindset*

ANNE DRYBURGH

The Emotionally Abusive Parent

Its Effects And How To Overcome Them In Christ

Illumine Press

United Kingdom

COPYRIGHT © Anne Dryburgh, 2021

The moral right of the author has been asserted.

ISBN: 978-1-7398719-0-1 (paperback)

ISBN: 978-1-7398719-1-8 (e-book)

Some people stand out because of their lifestyle of hospitality and caring for others. This book is dedicated to David & Jackie Clarke and Peter & Jocelyn Anderson who live such lives.

Special thanks also to Lou Priolo and Fraser Keay for their generous help with the editing process. Thanks to their help, this is a much better book.

About Anne

ANNE DRYBURGH, PH.D., is a biblical counselor certified by the *Association of Certified Biblical Counselors* (ACBC), the *International Association of Biblical Counselors* (IABC), and *The Addiction Connection*, a collective of biblical counselors and ministries united for the purpose of training and equipping the body of Christ in biblically helping addicts and their loved ones. She has been a missionary with *Echoes International* in Flemish-speaking Belgium since the 1990s. She coordinates *Reigning Grace Institute Europe* and is a team member of *Overseas Instruction in Counseling*. She is also on the adjunct faculty of the *Strengthening Ministries Training Institute* in South Africa. Anne serves on the advisory board of *Fallen Soldiers March* and is an external reader for doctoral candidates at the *Master's International University of Divinity*. She is the author of *Debilitated and Diminished: Help for Women in Emotionally Abusive Marriages*, and *(Un)ashamed: Christ's Transforming Hope for Rape Victims*.

Contents

Foreword

PEOPLE EXPERIENCE LIFE in a variety of ways. That's an understatement. Narrow those experiences to family life and you still get a wide array of experiences. For many, they have fond memories of their family life and are inexorably thankful for their family and the experiences they had growing up. In stark contrast, there are those who are indelibly hurt by their family. They were hurt physically, abandoned, or left to fend for themselves without any care or provision. These types of hurts in a family, however, are more noticeable than those that derive from what is referred to as emotional abuse. Gravely, multitudes of people have grown up in families, experiencing years of such abuse. They need help making sense of their experience and how to respond to it.

Emotional abuse is a term that can be easily misunderstood and as a result, misused. The time for clarity is now. And the time to provide help is now. Anne Dryburgh is an excellent person to address this issue and help us see with the clarity of Scripture what emotional abuse is, how to perceive it, and how to respond to it in a healthy and God glorifying way. Combined with her command of Scripture, Scottish wit, and abundant experience helping people navigate these troubling circumstances, Anne provides us with a sympathetic, compassionate, and hope-giving resource to help people rightly understand and respond to their experiences of emotional abuse.

Anne walks us through a biblical understanding of emotional abuse and its impact on the thinking, behavior, and emotions of those who have experienced it. With remarkable insight, she unpacks for us the devastating effect emotional abuse can have on others, helping us understand those impacted by it much better. From there she skillfully directs our attention to God and his Word. We see emotional abuse and its impact through the lens of Scripture, giving us a theological perspective on these experiences. Every step of the way, with forthright, relevant, and clear teaching, Anne leads us toward practical approaches to thinking and responding rightly. She is candid about the issues and boldly proclaims the hope of Christ to help those who have experienced emotional abuse at the hands of their parents.

I am grateful for Anne Dryburgh's love for the hurting, her tireless labor to draw the hurting to Christ, and her spirited desire to see God transform people's lives. All of that comes through powerfully in this book. I pray that God will use it mightily for his glory and for the good of thousands.

Andrew Rogers, PhD, Executive Director, Overseas Instruction in Counseling

Introduction

Unconditional, undying love. No matter what their children do, or how bad they become, parents give their lives for their children and protect them from all harm. Mothers and fathers sacrifice themselves to ensure that their children make it in life and grow and develop to do better than they did.

W AS THAT YOUR experience growing up? Have you heard people say that it is malicious to claim that a parent doesn't love their child when you know that was true in your own life?

Sadly, for many, when they think of a parent what comes to mind is someone vindictive, harmful, and scary; someone who insulted, demeaned, and tried to destroy them. A person who was filled with jealousy, bitterness, anger, and was cruel. Many children have been told, or it was made clear to them, that they are inadequate and have no right to exist. Hearing these things as they grew up affected how they viewed themselves and all areas of life. This is what many refer to as emotional or psychological abuse. Has this been your personal experience?

What this book is not

Since this is a short book not every question concerning parental emotional abuse could possibly be addressed. It cannot cover every practical issue you may be facing, nor does it present all the Bible teaches on the subject since that would take a much longer book.

How this book can help you

Instead, the aim of this book is to help you realize that if you have suffered parental emotional abuse, you *can* live in the truth that in Christ you have everything you need for life and godliness (2 Peter 1:3; Ephesians 1:3). In Christ you have everything, including everything for dealing with your childhood experiences. That sounds crazy when you think of the suffering you may have endured as you were growing up. It also sounds crazy when the lasting effects clearly impacted who you are, but this book will help you discover how you can live out this profound truth.

We will learn what secularists refer to as emotional abuse, how to understand it biblically, what it looks like in how a parent relates to a child, and at the effects on the child. As we look at these effects, we will also look at what is true about being in Christ and how you can live on the basis of who you are in him. We will also meet Laura in several of the chapters, hear about what she suffered, and how she learned to see who she is in Christ and deal graciously with her parent.

1. What is Emotional Abuse?

MANY YEARS AGO I went to the doctor because my knee was hurting really badly. I was used to playing sports, but I found that I couldn't even kneel or stand straight. The pain was excruciating. Confident that he knew the cause of my problem, the doctor said it was my meniscus (a small C-shaped piece of tissue in the knee which acts like a shock absorber) and he prescribed pain killers and physiotherapy. The excruciating pain continued despite following the doctor's instructions. Eventually, I went to another doctor who discovered that the problem was related to how my knee cap functioned: it had nothing to do with the meniscus.

When we try and work on things in life, it is essential we correctly understand the problem. If we get the diagnosis wrong, as my first doctor did, we won't find the correct solution. To help you live as God intends after growing up in an emotionally abusive home, it's essential to first understand what is known as emotional abuse and what the effects usually are for the children. After we've done that, we briefly examine how the Holy Spirit can help you now that you are in Christ.

The secular world understands that some parents

mistreat their children in abusive ways. What is known as 'emotional abuse', which some call psychological mistreatment, is "a repeated pattern of caregiver behavior or a serious incident that transmits to the child that s/he is worthless, flawed, unloved, unwanted, endangered, or only of value in meeting another's needs."[1]

What does this look like in how the parent relates to their child? Author Elizabeth Hopper provides a helpful list of ways that emotionally abusive parents treat their children:

The parent:

1. Calls the child derogatory names, ridicules, scolds, blames, humiliates, verbally attacks, or belittles the child.

2. Displays an ongoing pattern of negativity or hostility toward the child; examples are refusing to talk to the child, giving hateful looks, and undermining the child for who they are, their gender, and what they do.

3. Makes excessive and/or inappropriate demands of the child.

4. Exposes the child to extreme or unpredictable caregiver behaviors.

5. Uses fear, intimidation, humiliation, threats, or bullying to discipline the child or pressures the

---

1 Elizabeth Hopper, Frances Grossman, Joseph Spinazzola & Marla Zucker. *Treating Adult Survivors of Childhood Emotional Abuse and Neglect: Component-Based Psychotherapy* (New York: The Guilford Press, 2019), p 3.

child to keep secrets. The parent may threaten abandonment and/or exposing the child to situations that are scary and overwhelming.

6. Demonstrates a pattern of boundary violations, excessive monitoring, or overcontrol that is inappropriate considering the child's age.

7. Expects the child to assume an inappropriate level of responsibility or places them in role reversal, such as frequently taking care of younger siblings or attending to the emotional needs of the caregiver.

8. Undermines the child's significant relationships.

9. Does not allow the child to engage in age-appropriate socialization.[2]

Laura's story

Laura watched how the young mothers cared for their kids at small group. It was strange to see how families related to each other as she waited in vain for put downs and insults. They were characterized by love, encouragement, acceptance, and care, even when the children misbehaved. Throughout her life, Laura's mother had humiliated, blamed, and made fun of her. Her mother was always angry and critical, while expecting her to never make a mistake.

She tried everything she could to make her mother happy and to be accepted by her, but nothing worked. Nothing was good enough. Even when she tried her hardest to be who her mother wanted, she was made fun of in front

<hr>

2 Hopper, Grossman, Spinazzola & Zucker. p 4.

of others. Laura was scared to make a wrong move. Her mother had threatened her many times with punishment if she ever caused shame to the family. She checked up on her all the time, even demanding to know everything when Laura was in her 20s. Each time Laura made new friends, even as an adult, her mother would turn them against her.

Questions For Reflection

1. Which types of behavior in Hopper's list can you identify with?

2. Which sort of emotionally abusive behavior would you add?

2. Taking a Closer Look

PATRICIA WAS MY childhood friend. Her mother, Diane, was consumed with what people thought about her. If Diane was not the center of attention and seen to be the most important, Patricia had to pay. Diane was madly jealous of her younger sister who had married a university professor, while her husband was 'only' a repair man. When asked what his occupation was, Diane would say that he was a maintenance engineer and even had this written on Patricia's birth certificate.

When Patricia's friends would visit, Diane made them drink from china cups, instead of the usual mugs. I can clearly remember the day when Diane scolded Patricia when she innocently asked why they were drinking from the china tea set. Patricia told me later she was punished because Diane wanted her friends to think they always used expensive china cups.

Patricia had to excel at school, which she did, but was then punished for either not being good enough or being 'too big for her boots' (behaving as if you are more important than you really are). If she got some kind of commendation, Diane would mock her, and the older sibling would join in. If Diane were caught gossiping about someone, she would blame it on Patricia, causing people to think badly of her and shun her. I remember each time that Patricia would make new friends, Diane would make fun of Patricia. Most of them stopped hanging out with her.

If you, as with Patricia's case, grew up in an emotionally abusive home, image will have been all-important to your parent. You would have had to behave in such a way that their (false) image about themselves was portrayed to the outside world, ensuring that others believed that they were a good person who could never be given criticism, blame, or shamed in any way. They believed that they were superior and should be treated accordingly.

You were the one who had to provide fulfillment and ensure that they received adoration and control. If someone spoke to them about something that they had said or done, they would have become intensely angry, which may have sometimes spilled over into full-blown rage. You were prevented from developing into adulthood and they became jealous if you achieved something or got attention instead of them. To be able to do this, your parent controlled you and told you what to believe and how to behave.

How do they go about it?

Emotionally abusive parents are manipulative, keep information from you, accuse you of being or doing what the parent is being or doing, and talk to someone else about you instead of talking to you directly. They put you down, refuse to take responsibility, don't speak to you for periods of time, and ignore you. They twist what you think and feel, humiliate you in front of others by making fun of you, slander you to others, undermine you, minimize what you think and do, and mock you. When they are portraying themselves as a good person to others, they communicate concern about their troubled child, giving the impression that you are problematic.

It has been observed that there are four layers to the behavior of emotionally abusive mothers. These are:

1. *Admiration.* This is their attitude to life. They want and expect to be admired, listened to, and agreed with.
2. *Fear.* If people do not admire them, they will try to make them become fearful. At this point they will enter into what is known as narcissistic rage.[3]
3. *Pity.* If fear does not work, they will try to gain other people's pity by playing the victim.
4. *Vindictiveness.* If pity does not work, they will become vindictive and start a smear campaign.[4]

Many abusive parents engage in what are known as the three D's: drama, denial, and deflection.

---

3 The Bible does not use the word "narcissist," but it does address the motives and behaviors that are involved. According to the Bible, narcissism is insolent pride. For more information see https://biblicalperspectivesonnarcissism.com/2018/12/06/narcissism-insolent-pride-in-the-bible/

4 Danu Morrigan, *You're Not Crazy – It's Your Mother* (London: Darton, Longman, and Todd Ltd, 2012), p 38. (as with other cited sources, the author does not agree with or endorse all that the writer teaches).

1. **Drama:** If they are challenged or criticized, they will react in a dramatic way.
2. **Denial:** If drama does not work, they will deny that they had said or done what they are being challenged about. The parent will say that you did not see what you saw, that you are imagining things, or that you are dreaming.
3. **Deflection:** If denial does not work, they will engage in deflection. For example, if they are faced with criticism, or are challenged, they will change the topic onto the person who is criticizing them. In the process, the discussion becomes about the other person's faults and shortcomings, instead of the issue that was raised. By doing this, they do not have to admit that *they* have done wrong.

If these do not work, they might say that they are sorry, but do so in a way that puts the blame on you. Examples are "I am sorry you can't take a joke," or "I am sorry that you got upset." If they apologize in this way, they expect that life goes on as if nothing has happened. However, if they think that you have done something wrong, they make you apologize until they find the level of the apology acceptable enough.[5]

---

5 Another strategy is what is known as DARVO, an acronym for Deny, Attack, Reverse, Victim and Offender. The perpetrator may *Deny* the behavior, *Attack* the individual doing the confronting, and *Reverse* the roles of *Victim* and *Offender* with the result that the perpetrator then becomes the victim and the victim the perpetrator. For more information see: https://medium.com/narcissistic-abuse-rehab/how-narcissists-use-darvo-to-escape-accountability-f0cb48708010

Questions For Reflection

1. In what ways did your parent express the four layers of emotional abuse?

2. Think about how your parent responded to criticism. In what ways did they express the three D's?

3. General Impact

On behavior

MRS. CARMICHAEL WAS a living demonstration of how making sure someone is happy with you directly impacts your behavior. I was 7 years old, and it was back in the day when school teachers punished badly behaved pupils by hitting them with a leather belt. The normal procedure was for kids to hold out their hands, palms up, and then they would be struck. Mrs. Carmichael had her own method of instilling us with fear. She would belt people with the palms down, across the fingers. Just the thought of being belted in this way kept us in constant fear, and her happy. We were the best-behaved class in the school.

This childhood example shows how the way that adults treat us impacts our behavior. This is especially true of the effect of the parent-child relationship.

Under/Over performing

You might struggle in the area of performance. On the one hand, you have been raised to believe that you are incapable of doing anything and therefore unable to achieve things in life. You might struggle with the fear of failure and postpone things that you think you are not capable of doing. This can lead to serious problems in your workplace, marriage, education, and parenting.

At the same time, you have been raised to ensure that your parent is well thought of. Your achievements are not for yourself, but for your parent's reputation. You might believe that by doing well, you can win your parent's love and acceptance, but sadly, this never happens. Even though your parent made you perform so that they were well thought of by others, you could never become better than, or become better thought of, than your parent. Even into adulthood, you could still be too fearful to do anything you believe your parent would not approve of. This mindset of overachieving to 'become' someone, could mean that you still try to outperform others.

The inclination to under- or over-achieve can be changed as you let the Lord work on your motives. Your motive in life as a believer is to glorify God. This includes how you do your work. Rather than trying to be better than other people, to be the best so that you are the most important, or fearing failure and therefore under-achieving, you can learn to do all to glorify the Lord.

> *And whatever you do, in word or deed, do every-thing in the name of the Lord Jesus, giving thanks to God the Father through him (Colossians 3:17).*

> *So, whether you eat or drink, or whatever you do, do all to the glory of God (1 Corinthians 10:31).*

The change in motivation is from what your parent will think and how they will respond, to glorifying the Lord as you trust that your reputation depends on the Lord. You can learn to be responsible to the Lord for how you live, think, behave, relate, and deal with your emotions and come to understand that you are not responsible for your parent, to your parent, or for their reputation.

As you do all for the glory of God, you can relate to others for their good as you love the Lord and others (Matthew 22:37-39). Loving others does not mean pleasing them, rather *relating* to them for their good, as the Lord defines good.

Dealing with your heart will help you when others succeed, and you don't. Other people succeeding does not mean that you are a failure. Who you are as a person depends on God and who he says that you are, not on what you achieve or what others think of you. Living in this way will also help you to deal with any tendency toward pride and jealousy when you succeed or fail.

Fearful in relationships

You will have grown up living in fear. It probably became part of who you are and how you relate to other people. As an adult, you might run from close relationships, close yourself off emotionally, or become aggressive toward others.

In social settings, you could fear being judged and might second-guess people. You could struggle to voice and stick to your opinion and wishes, cope with confrontation, say no, show your emotions, and to trust others.

Since you find trusting others hard, you will probably be scared to share your thoughts and opinions, even with people who are kind to you. Your experience in life has been that being vulnerable in this way has resulted in mockery, hurt, and abandonment. You might fear that those who mean the most to you in your adult life will do the same if you open up and are vulnerable with them. You might try to keep a safe distance from them until you are sure that you are safe. If you do dare to share something, your heightened sense of awareness means that you sense any sign of rejection or mockery. When you sense this, you will probably withdraw back to your safe place. Or you could become aggressive and try to insult and intimidate people. It's likely that you will continue to believe that people cannot be trusted and that it is better if you protect yourself. It could seem strange to you if people express interest in you for who you are, and it might take time for you to see that their interest is genuine.

Your fearfulness in relationships will be changed as you live according to who God says that you are, let him change your heart, and begin relating to others in ways that honor him and are for their good. It's crucial that you learn how to communicate, appropriately say no at times, and build healthy relationships. Your trust is in the Lord, and it is from your trust in him that you relate to others. To gain his wisdom for how to relate to people, you could read *Proverbs* and learn what it means to be discerning and wise, instead of foolish.

Trust can only be given to people based on their character, not because they demand it by making comments such as "you must trust me 100%," or try to make you feel guilty for not giving it. Anyone who says these things is showing that they are manipulative, and their trustworthiness is questionable. You can learn to trust people gradually, based on how well you know them and how they treat you. More aspects about relating to others will be covered later in the book.

Relating to others in order to win love and approval

Were you raised to believe that you could win the love and approval of your parents by trying hard enough? This is a lie. Longing for your parent's love and approval will cause you to keep trying, even into adulthood, believing that your parent will be different at some point. You believe that their lack of love for you is due to a failure on your part in some way, perhaps your looks, weight, academic accomplishments, occupation, and/or gender. Your longing is for your parent to give you the love, support, care, and guidance that you crave. It is highly unlikely this will ever happen, so it is foolish to keep trying.

In your adult relationships, you might be inclined to relate to others who treat you in a similar way as your parents did. You might be compliant so that the other person does not become angry and aggressive, hoping that they will love and accept you. You could also be taken advantage of by others if they see that you will do anything to help and be liked. You could have taken on some of your parent's traits, such as always having to be right, feeling entitled, expecting others to submit to your thinking, not being able to receive criticism, and expecting perfection in others. Later in the book we will examine how you can learn to relate to people.

Self-harm

You might have engaged in self-harm when you were upset because of how your parent treated you. Examples of self-harm behaviors are disordered eating, cutting, and burning yourself. When you engage in these behaviors, your focus is on yourself and trying to alleviate your emotional pain. By better understanding what you are experiencing, such as anger, depression, hurt, and rejection, you can learn to deal with your heart. You can do this by learning to become aware of what you are thinking throughout the day about yourself, your life, and others in your life. We will look at how to do this shortly.

As you see what is going on in your mind, you can submit those thoughts to what is true about yourself, your life, and others, according to the Lord. You will then be living according to what is true about God, who you are as a person, and others and how they treat you.

Addiction

If your desire to be loved, wanted, and accepted is thwarted and mocked, it is incredibly painful to bear. You could experience the pain of rejection, believe that you are inferior to others, and think that you are inadequate. These emotions are so strong that you might be tempted to do something, indulge in something, to feel better. Many people who experience this become addicts. Common addictions include alcohol, drugs, food, and sex.

To live as God intends, you will need to know who God is and who you are in him. This will help you deal with your painful emotions. To do this, it's important for you to become aware of what you think and how you respond to the people and events in your life. A way of doing this is for you to write down what you are thinking when you are upset. You could take a note of who you were with, or who it was about, what you were doing, and where you were. By doing this, you will see what you are believing about yourself and the people and events that encourage those beliefs.

Addicts will almost certainly indulge in their substance if the three A's of anonymity, availability, and appetite are available. If you are on your own, your addiction of choice is available, and you have the desire to use, you will most likely succumb to it. It's helpful for you to structure your life in such a way that you make it as difficult as possible to practice your addiction. This will include being alone as little as possible by having people in your life who know what you are doing and to whom you are accountable. It will include blocking availability of the substance as much as is possible, such as not having alcohol in the house, having filters on the internet, having accountability partners on the internet, and having someone with you when you buy food. As you deal with your heart and mind, you will be dealing with the appetite that you have for your substance.

Passivity

You might have come to a point of believing that what you do doesn't matter, that you have little or no influence in life. This can result in you becoming passive and living in a sort of helpless state. But as you learn to live for the glory of God, you will see that your life does matter. Your purpose in life is to be holy and blameless before God (Ephesians 1:4). Your life matters because you were chosen in Christ before the foundation of the world.

Laura's story

Despite longing to be loved and accepted, Laura did all that she could to keep others at bay. When people tried to get close to her, she would run from them, close herself off emotionally, or insult and try to intimidate them. In her mind, people couldn't be trusted since they reject and hurt you. Laura knew that she had to protect herself.

When she was with others, Laura tried to figure out what they were thinking and what they would do, so that she was a step ahead of them and knew how to respond. She struggled to let other people know what her opinion was about something because she was used to being laughed at for her views.

Then, Laura started to write down what she was thinking before she had to spend time with a group of people. She became aware of when she thought that others would mock her, exclude her, or reject her. Since her desire was to honor the Lord, she learned to think about herself and the other people she was with according to the Bible. Instead of focusing on herself, she would seek ways to show interest in others. When she had the opportunity to give her opinion on a given topic, she learned to say to herself that their reaction is their responsibility before God and does not mean that her opinion is foolish.

Questions For Reflection

1. What do you often think about while you are working? How could you replace that with thoughts that honor the Lord?

2. Read through the book of Proverbs. What do you discover about being wise and discerning when relating to others?

3. When you are upset, what do you do to help make yourself feel better?

4. Impact on Thinking

EVER SINCE SEEING his parents fight when he was a kid, Kevin lived in fear of something happening to him. When tensions rose at home, he would "zone out" (become oblivious to his own surroundings) because the tension he experienced in the home was too much for him. As he grew up, his parents would mock him, put him down, criticize him, and insult him. After a while, he would zone out during family gatherings because he felt uncomfortable. The other family members thought he was odd and rude, believing that his behavior showed that he was spoiled. Kevin would later zone out at school and later in the workplace. Not only did he get into trouble at work because of his poor work performance, he had few friends because he lacked social skills and came across as rude and disinterested in others.

Concentration

Growing up in a home where you did not learn to be responsible for your thinking, means you could experience difficulty concentrating. A helpful way to learn to concentrate and focus is to think and work in ways that honor God (1 Corinthians 10:31; Colossians 3:17). When you become aware that your thoughts have drifted, you can then bring them back to what is in front of you. Since you might have struggled with concentration all of your life, this will probably take time to learn.

Intrusive thoughts

Memories of shaming and humiliating moments can intrusively come into your thinking. Afterwards, you might be upset and be left suffering with a sense of shame.

Disengaged thinking (technical term: dissociation)

A way that you may have coped growing up was by disengaging from your thinking so that you are separated from an awareness of your surroundings. You then become emotionally numb. Disengaging can include daydreaming, transporting yourself to a fantasy location, entering into pretend events, switching off from following conversations, and "spacing out." These affect your ability to concentrate, do your job, have healthy relationships, sleep, and perform daily activities.

We have seen that your purpose in life is to glorify Christ, and central to this is a mind that honors him. In Ephesians 4:17-24 we read:

> Now this I say and testify in the Lord, that you must no longer walk as the Gentiles do, in the

futility of their minds. They are darkened in their understanding, alienated from the life of God because of the ignorance that is in them, due to their hardness of heart. They have become callous and have given themselves up to every kind of impurity. But that is not the way that you have learned Christ – assuming that you have heard about him and were taught in him, as the truth [that] is in Jesus, to put off your old self, which belongs to your former manner of life and is corrupt through deceitful desires, and to be renewed in the spirit of your minds, and to put on the new self, created after the likeness of God in true righteousness and holiness.

According to this passage, the way that an abusive parent thinks is futile: they are darkened in their understanding due to the ignorance that is in them because of the hardness of their heart. It is alienated from the life of God. This way of thinking is typical of the unbeliever; outside of Christ you will have thought like this as well. If your parent *is* a Christian, they are still thinking in futile ways and not according to the mind of Christ.

It's crucial that you transform your thinking from the influence of your parent's futile and darkened mindset and that you are renewed in the spirit of your mind (Romans 12:2; Colossians 3:1-2).

Practically, this will involve bringing all your desires, thoughts, and beliefs into alignment with what is true in Scripture. You can test all that your parent, and others, have said to you about who you are and how to live, according to what the Lord teaches. Rather than accepting what they say, you can learn to renew your mind and think according to what is true in Scripture. This includes accusations, insinuations, exaggerations, twisting of facts, and attempts to make you feel guilty.

If you disengage your thinking, or have intrusive thoughts about the past, you can learn to focus on what is real, your present location, and who is with you. If you keep a note of when you experience intrusive thoughts, you can see if it was at a specific time of day, around the time of certain events, if they happened indoors or outdoors, or during a meal. It's a good idea for you to write down what was happening when the thoughts began and what you and the people with you were doing at the time. The next time you are in a similar situation, you can plan what you will think about and focus on. It would be helpful for you to write out and memorize relevant Bible verses or passages that you can take with you and read so that your thinking can be reoriented and brought back to reality and truth.

If you are tempted to disengage your thinking, it is crucial for you to do things to focus on the present. Examples of things that can be helpful are calling someone, listening to music, singing, or praying. You can also speak biblical truths out loud and look around you while taking note of all the things in the room and the colors that you see.

Questions For Reflection

1. When do your thoughts tend to drift? Take a note of these times and bring your thoughts back to what is in front of you.

2. In what ways do you disengage your thinking?

3. What have your parents said about you? In contrast, what does Scripture say?

5. Impact on Relating to Other People

J ESS NOT ONLY 'zoned out',[6] she also lived to be loved and accepted by others, even as an adult. I remember seeing this clearly with her baking business.

Whenever she baked a cake, it had to be better than anyone else's. So much so, that other people started to resent the way that she had to be the center of attention and better than them. The next time she met someone who had tasted some of her baking, she would repeatedly ask them how good the baking was, if they liked it, and if they thought she was a good baker. When someone gave any kind of correction, or said that they did not like it, Jess's world fell apart and she went to bed for the rest of the day. Who she was, was dependent on whether other people thought she was the best at baking. If she was not, it meant that she was a failure.

Boundaries

When you were a child, you will not have learned to be responsible for yourself, nor how to ask for what you

---

6 Temporarily stop paying attention to what you can see or hear around you.

need in appropriate ways. It could be that despite now being an adult you still have the tendency to people-please. To be able to understand and relate to people, it's important for you to see when people are trying to manipulate you and to speak up.

You could ask yourself why it is that you want to do something. Is it because you believe that it honors the Lord, or is it to please someone? If you feel offended by someone, is it because that was their intention, or are you perhaps reacting to the emotions and reactions of others? If you think that you are being rejected, ask yourself if this is the case or are the people involved choosing to spend time with someone else? If you are being left out and excluded, it will be helpful to fill your mind with who you are in Christ. Who you are depends on the Lord and not on other people and how they treat you. Who you are remains the same forever – nobody can affect this in any way.

As you were growing up, you may have been called selfish for doing things that your parent did not want you to do. It is important that you learn to first glorify the Lord in your thinking and behaviors as you take up your responsibilities, and from there to think about how you can love others. It would be easy for you to continue to give your parent whatever they want because you do not want to be selfish as you know you are to die to self and love and honor your parent.

Sometimes your parent, or other well-meaning believers, will proof text the verse "honor your father and your mother" (Ephesians 6:2) as a way to try to get you to ensure that your parent is happy with you and that *their* feelings are not hurt. However, honoring your parent is not about ensuring that they are happy, it is about making sure that they are taken care of. This can be seen in 1 Timothy 5:3-8, where Paul urges believers to care for their widowed mothers. Taking care of parents can be done in different ways, such as ensuring that they have carers at their home or residential/care home when due to old age they can no longer look after themselves. It does not necessarily mean that you have your parent live with you or you become their full-time carer.

It is helpful to ask whether giving the parent what they want is honoring to the Lord. Does it come from a place where you are glorifying the Lord as someone new in Christ? Are you responding out of fear? Would it mean succumbing to sinful behavior on the parent's part, such as the use of intimidation and threats? Would it lead to coming under the parent's control? Would it be detrimental to fulfilling your God-given responsibilities, such as your marriage, your children, your home, the care of your body, friendships, and the use of time? Honoring your parent does not mean that you are to accept and tolerate sinful treatment that is harmful to you and other family members.

If you have since become a parent yourself, you are also called to protect any children of your own from being sinned against and harmed. This means that you may need to think through how much exposure you give your child(ren) to an abusive parent.

Observe, not absorb

Learning to communicate will also help you with your future relationships. If you have suffered emotional abuse, it is less likely you will have been taught to be a responsible adult who can make your own choices. Saying 'No' to someone who is demanding seemed like something impossible to do as you grew up. Since it was and may still be unthinkable for you to say 'No', your parent will continue to be demanding and intruding in adulthood.

As you grow stronger, learning to live out who you already are in Christ, you can be helped to think about communicating to your parent that change will be coming in some areas. Examples are how the parent speaks, relates to you and your family, and your involvement in private family matters. Is it acceptable for your parent to come unannounced to your house, read your emails, open your mail, and know details about your everyday life? Areas where change can come are when the parent insults, demeans, ridicules, threatens, controls, or shouts at you because these behaviors are sinful and do not glorify God.

If your parent verbally attacks you, you could say to them that you want your conversation together to be calm and productive, not one in which you attack each other verbally. You could ask them to stop speaking to you in that way. If the parent continues to do so, you could repeat what you have just said and add that the parent will have to leave the house (or that you will have to leave the house or the other place where you are speaking), or that you will stop speaking on the phone if they do not stop. If, when discussing an issue with the parent, they start to verbally attack you, accuse you, blame you, or divert the conversation onto something else, instead of being diverted, becoming defensive, or retaliating, it is important that you stick to the issue being discussed by repeating what you were talking about in a polite and calm way.

It is to be expected that your parent will not respond well to being told 'No'. They might start to behave in an extreme way to force you to back down. You can expect them to react with anger, rage, self-pity, crying, making threats, slander, revenge, ostracism, or rejection. They may even make suicidal comments, such as, "If you don't let me come and visit, I will kill myself" or "My life will have no meaning if I can't come and visit you everyday." It's crucial that you do not back down and give in, even though the pressure can be intense.

You could choose to keep conversations on super-ficial topics. This will help ensure that your parent is not able to gain an emotional hold. With time, you can learn to react without emotion. Remember, it is your emotional reaction that feeds them. This means that you learn to observe what your parent is saying and doing but not absorb it. This involves watching them to try to understand what is behind their behavior, which will help you come to see through their manipulation and not give in to it.

Another aspect is to communicate factually with them, not emotionally, and without explanation. You don't need to explain your reasons for your choices to them. If you do, they will only be contested. You do not need to win your parent's approval for your choices or what you do.

It's likely that your parent will send other people to get you to do what they want. They might come with good intentions, telling you how your parent misses you and is broken by how they are being treated. They might reprimand you for being selfish and not honoring your parent and then proceed to tell you what they think you should be doing as a good son or daughter. In these situations, you can observe and not absorb what is being said so that you are able to discern what is going on.

People-pleasing

You may have grown up to need the love, approval, and praise of others to validate who you are as a person. Living like this will mean you remain dependent on others for who you are as a person. You might seek validation from friends, family members, partners, and coworkers. This may be done in an attempt to feel safe and looked after and out of fear of rejection, believing that if you do not do what people want, or say no to others, they will reject you.

If you do experience love and care, you could start to cling to that person as you are getting a sense of self and identity from them. This could get to the point of being unbearable for the other person, resulting in them breaking ties with you. This broken relationship will confirm to you that you are unlovable. Although you long to be loved and cared for, actually *experiencing* it may be terrifying, resulting in you remaining distant in relationships and not letting people in. You could also sabotage relationships when people start to become emotionally close to you because you are fearful of being hurt. You might feel comfortable when you perceive yourself as being seen, and as being the most important, but you will fall apart when you are ignored or left out.

This inherent people-pleasing may also be seen in your behavior in the workplace. In an attempt to be respected, liked, and approved, you might be inclined to work very hard, work during vacations, and be willing to help in any way that you can. Knowing that you are willing to do anything will mean that it is likely that you will be taken advantage of and never promoted.

Responsible for others' emotions

Having been raised to be responsible for the parent's emotional well-being, you could have developed a high sensitivity to the emotions and reactions of others. It's likely that you are very sensitive to when another person is moody, in a huff, or disapproves. You will probably believe that you are responsible for making the person feel better and may believe that it is your fault if they are upset. You fear rejection, being punished, and/or being ostracized. If you are married, you could make your partner's problems your own and, in the process, become overwhelmed.

While learning to live as who you are in Christ, it is essential that you learn that you are responsible for your own emotions, not those of other people. While it is right for you to be concerned for them, if you take their responsibilities upon yourself, it will result in frustration, anger, and fear. The Lord does not give you the resources for other people's responsibilities, and because of that you are not equipped to manage them. It would be helpful for you to study the "one anothers" of Scripture to discover how to relate to others. These can be found by a simple search on the internet.

Behave like the parent

When we are children, we believe that our parents are right and the standard by which to behave. They know right from wrong. We absorb and emulate our parents in our thinking and behavior. It is to be expected that you will have areas in your life where you think and behave like your parent. You might get very angry, be abusive in how you speak, be arrogant, hostile to others, demand attention from others, expect your opinion to be worshipped, not be able to accept someone disagreeing with you, and reject others.

But change comes as you learn to deal with your heart and live according to who you are in Christ. Your thinking will change from seeing others from a self-centered and entitled perspective, to seeing other people as those made in the image of God, and who are full of his dignity (Genesis 1:26-28). If the other people are believers, they are also fellow members of the family of God (John 1:12). You can change to thinking about how you can bless others by relating to them in a way that honors the Lord and is for their good. This involves sacrificial servanthood.

When you see that you have related selfishly, you can confess and ask for forgiveness for sinning against them. You will see that your opinion is not more important than other people's, and can learn to listen lovingly to them. Your speaking will change from self-serving, attacking, and self-preserving to seeking to speak in a helpful and loving way (Ephesians 4:15, 29; James 3:5-11; 4:11; Galatians 5:19-26).

Isolation

You may have become isolated because of the belief that you are unlovable. Isolation is also a way to keep others from finding out about your abusive past. If you have withdrawn, you will have few friendships. This is where the two greatest commandments have special significance – to love the Lord with all your being and your neighbor as you already love yourself (Matthew 22:36-39). If you have withdrawn into isolation, your focus is on yourself. But by loving the Lord and other people, you become outward focused. You can look to how to love and be a blessing to others by thinking what you can do that would be helpful for them. Looking up all the references to "one another" in Scripture – I mentioned this before – will give you insights into what this involves. You can then think and pray about how to apply these principles in a practical way for the benefit of others.

At the same time, you are called to mature as a

believer. To grow as a believer, it would be helpful for you to seek older godlier people to learn from who can be models for you about how to be a Christian (Titus 2:2-5) in every area of your life.

Laura's story

Laura had to learn to limit the influence her mother had on her and her family. She started out by choosing to stay calm and observe her mother so that she could see what she was saying and doing. This made it possible for her to notice when her mother was trying to manipulate her. When her mother started to berate or mock her, Laura said that she wanted to talk with her, but not in that way. For example, "I want to talk with you, but not in a way where one person pulls down the other."

Every time that her mother started to speak in that manner, Laura calmly repeated the same statement. Her mother usually responded with anger and further mockery. Each time she did that, Laura again repeated her statement and then would leave the room or end the phone call.

Laura realized that her way of relating to others had been protective; she was focused on herself. She noted every time that she had a fearful thought, or when she thought that she was being rejected. She would ask herself if the sense of fear and rejection was based on evidence, or if it was her reaction coming from experiences in her past.

Laura asked, "How can I honor the Lord toward this person in my reaction?" She began to choose to invest in people, showing an interest in their lives and looking for ways of doing good to them. She worked hard on her tendency to want to please people so that she would be loved and accepted. If someone left her out, she stopped herself thinking that she was inadequate and therefore needed to make other people feel good for her to be acceptable.

Questions For Reflection

1. When your parent asks something from you, how do you respond? Do you concede to keep the peace?

2. In what ways do you relate to others as your parent does?

3. In what ways can you show interest in others and help them in practical ways?

6. Impact on Emotions

IT WAS GLEN who showed me the impact that emotionally abusive parents can have on their adult children. He shared with me about the time he went to visit his abusive father. Even though he was in his 40s, the whole experience was very upsetting for him. When Glen asked why his father had said something that was untrue about him, his father lashed out and called Glen names and spoke about what a complete failure he was. When he left, Glen felt numb. The next day he struggled to get out of bed because he felt unwanted and, as he was such a failure, wondered what the point was of doing anything. Glen continued sharing about how he thought about aspects of who God is, especially that he is in control of his life. It is the Lord who chose him, is in control of his life, and who is the purpose of his life. Thinking about who the Lord is helped bring him out of being emotionally distraught, to living intentionally and in life-giving truth.

Sensitive to others

Are you easily affected by other people's moods and words? Do you avoid anything that you consider to be negative emotion, such as anger or sadness, or positive emotion, such as joy and hope? If you are confronted with anger, do you become fearful and withdraw into yourself? Are you too timid to share what you think, and do you tend to give in to others in order to keep the peace? Do you believe that you are responsible for making sure there is peace? When you are with others who are happy, or experience happiness yourself, is it a scary experience for you since you expect that it won't last? If another person becomes more emotional than you can handle, do you struggle with hyperarousal? (This is "an abnormal state of increased responsiveness to stimuli that is marked by various physiological and psychological symptoms, such as increased levels of alertness and anxiety and elevated heart rate and respiration.")[7] If this occurs, you will probably have problems concentrating, sleeping, be easily startled, and become hypervigilant – this where you become "highly alert to potential danger or threat".[8] Are you sensitive to criticism, rejection, and (perceived) abandonment? If this was your experience at home as you were growing up, you will probably be expecting it and looking for danger in other relationships.

Fear

Throughout this book we have spoken about being fearful of others. You might be living in an anxious state, being alert to how people could harm you, or you could become emotionally numb as a way to protect yourself.

---

7 https://www.merriam-webster.com/dictionary/hyperarousal
8 https://www.merriam-webster.com/dictionary/hypervigilant

You could be unsure about how to behave with others and be fearful of rejection and criticism.

If you became a parent yourself, you may have become fearful of being like your parent and harming your children, or of not being able to be a good parent. This belief is because you were raised to think that you were a failure and not capable of doing things in life. You will be different than your own parent as you live for the glory of God and become the parent the Lord calls you to be – dealing with your heart and raising your children to become people who also live for the glory of the Lord.

Dealing with fear and worry

As you deliberately think truth, you will begin to deal with thoughts filled with fear and worry since you are focusing your mind on who the Lord is. By meditating on who Christ is, and entrusting yourself to him, you can overcome your fear. Philippians 4:4-7 teaches specifically about how to overcome it.

> *Rejoice in the Lord always; again I will say, rejoice. Let your reasonableness be known to everyone. The Lord is at hand; do not be anxious about anything, but in everything by prayer and supplication with thanksgiving let your requests be made known to God. And the peace of God, which surpasses all understanding, will guard your hearts and your minds in Christ Jesus.*

Throughout the day, and especially when fearful thoughts come to mind, you should bring those thoughts to the Lord and then think about an attribute of God in relation to it. God's attributes are the characteristics of God that make up his nature. All his attributes form his character. If we mistakenly take only one of God's attributes apart from the others, it leads to misunderstanding. We look at some of these in the next chapter.

Questions For Reflection

1. How do you tend to respond to other people's emotions?

2. What kind of things are you fearful of?

7. Understanding Who God Is

God is omnipresent

GOD'S OMNIPRESENCE CAN be a tremendous help for you as you trust that he is with you wherever you go. You can know that wherever you are and whatever happens to you, as a believer, God is always with you. You are never alone.

> *"Am I a God at hand, declares the LORD, and not a God far away? Can a man hide himself in secret places so that I cannot see him? declares the LORD. Do I not fill heaven and earth? declares the LORD" (Jeremiah 23:23 24).*

> *Where shall I go from your Spirit?*

> *Or where shall I flee from your presence?*

> *If I ascend to heaven, you are there!*

> *If I make my bed in Sheol, you are there! If I take the wings of the morning and dwell in the uttermost parts of the sea, even there your hand shall lead me, and your right hand shall hold me (Psalm 139:7-10).*

Omniscient

As you work on dealing with fear and worry, you can trust God that he knows all things, including the answer to the mystery about why you were raised in an abusive home. You might want to know why you were born into such a family.

This understandable search for specific answers will be fruitless and possibly lead to more fear and confusion. It's important to see that the Lord knows all the details and aspects of your past life and your future. Focusing on this rather than living in fear or trying to take control yourself, is lifegiving. You might wonder where God was while you were growing up. It is crucial for you to know that the Lord will judge the evil abuse (see 'Full of Wrath' later on in this chapter).

> *For whenever our heart condemns us, God is greater than our heart, and he knows everything (1 John 3:20).*
>
> *O LORD, you have searched me and known me! You know when I sit down and when I rise up; you discern my thoughts from afar…*
>
> *Even before a word is on my tongue, behold, O LORD, you know it altogether…*
>
> *Your eyes saw my unformed substance; in your book were written, every one of them, the days that were formed for me, when as yet there was none of them (Psalm 139:1-2, 4, 16).*

Wise

Wisdom is found in Christ. The wisdom you need for how to make decisions, how to relate to people, and how to live in all areas of life is found in Scripture.

> *To the only wise God be glory forevermore through Jesus Christ! Amen (Romans 16:27).*

> *...but to those who are called, both Jews and Greeks, Christ the power of God and the wisdom of God...And because of him you are in Christ Jesus, who became to us wisdom from God, righteousness and sanctification and redemption (1 Corinthians 1:24, 30).*

> *...so that through the church the manifold wisdom of God might now be made known to the rulers and authorities in the heavenly places (Ephesians 3:10).*

> *...God's mystery, which is Christ, in whom are hidden all the treasures of wisdom and knowledge (Colossians 2:3).*

God is also...

Faithful

You have experienced abuse, deceit, and evil. In contrast, God is faithful. He is truthful. The Lord will keep his word and is true to his promises. As you recognize fears as they come up in your heart, remember what the Lord has said, and trust that he is true to his word. This is an excellent time to read real-life stories about people who have endured great suffering and have experienced the faithfulness of God throughout their lives. God is not just a rock; he is *the* Rock.

The Rock, his work is perfect, for all his ways are justice. A God of faithfulness and without iniquity, just and upright is he (Deuteronomy 32:4).

Good

You can know that God is good. There is no evil or wrongdoing in him. You know that people can be evil and cruel. But in contrast, God is good, and because of his goodness, the standard you should use for judging any behavior is God himself.

And Jesus said to him, "Why do you call me good? No one is good except God alone" (Luke 18:19).

For the LORD is good; his steadfast love endures forever, and his faithfulness to all generations (Psalm 100:5).

Praise the LORD! Oh give thanks to the LORD, for he is good, for his steadfast love endures forever! (Psalm 106:1).

Oh, taste and see that the LORD is good! Blessed is the one who takes refuge in him! (Psalm 34:8).

Loving

When dealing with your fears, you can know that God loves you, as he sent his Son to die for you. God is love and has expressed his love for you by sending his Son to die in your place. He acts in such a way toward you that it is for your benefit. You can trust that he will continue to love you and work in your life.

Anyone who does not love does not know God, because God is love (1 John 4:8).

For God so loved the world, that he gave his only Son, that whoever believes in him should not perish but have eternal life (John 3:16).

I have been crucified with Christ. It is no longer I who live, but Christ who lives in me. And the life I now live in the flesh I live by faith in the Son of God, who loved me and gave himself for me (Galatians 2:20).

Merciful

The Lord is compassionate toward you. He is kind and shows pity by ministering to you in your sadness and grief. You can be confident that he will continue to be compassionately merciful about your fears and about learning to trust him with your daily life.

Blessed be the God and Father of our Lord Jesus Christ, the Father of mercies and God of all comfort (2 Corinthians 1:3).

Gracious

It was because of his grace (unmerited favor) that God sent his Son to offer you salvation. Your relationship with the Lord has come about because of his grace. You can be sure that he will continue to be gracious to you. He will continue to extend unmerited favor toward you. As you trust him you begin to realize this more and more.

> ...and [you] are justified by his grace as a gift, through the redemption that is in Christ Jesus (Romans 3:24 – my insert).

> For you know the grace of our Lord Jesus Christ, that though he was rich, yet for your sake he became poor, so that you by his poverty might become rich (2 Corinthians 8:9).

> For by grace you have been saved through faith. And this is not your own doing; it is the gift of God (Ephesians 2:8).

Holy

When God is called holy, it means that he is unique. His nature is separate from that of his creation. He is morally pure and separate from evil. What happened to you is in direct contrast to his holiness. It was the opposite of God's character.

You can know that God can be trusted as he is morally pure. You can also know that the purpose of your own life is to become holy, which means that you are to become like Christ.

Whatever issues you fear and worry about, you can know that God is holy and that your purpose in life is to become like him. As you become Christ-like in your character, you will also remember his wisdom in making the necessary decisions you will face.

> *I will also praise you with the harp for your faithfulness, O my God; I will sing praises to you with the lyre, O Holy One of Israel (Psalm 71:22).*

> *For our shield belongs to the LORD, our king to the Holy One of Israel (Psalm 89:18).*

> *… it is written, "You shall be holy, for I am holy."* (1 Peter 1:16).

Righteous

Since God is holy, he is also righteous. And this righteousness is seen in what he does. You can trust that he will relate to you and guide you according to what is morally correct.

> *God is a righteous judge, and a God who feels indignation every day. (Psalm 7:11).*

Jealous

God being jealous means that he defends his character and reputation. You can trust that it is right and good for you to live in a way that honors him. As you trust God in your daily life, you can know you please him as you seek to honor him in all that you do.

For you shall worship no other god, for the LORD, whose name is Jealous, is a jealous God (Exodus 34:14).

For the LORD your God is a consuming fire, a jealous God (Deuteronomy 4:24).

You shall not make for yourself a carved image, or any likeness of anything that is in heaven above, or that is on the earth beneath, or that is in the water under the earth. You shall not bow down to them or serve them; for I the LORD your God am a jealous God, visiting the iniquity of the fathers on the children to the third and fourth generation of those who hate me (Deuteronomy 5:8-9).

Since he is jealous for his people, you can also be assured that he is jealous for you. God is committed to you through his covenant with you in Christ, and will work in your life for your good and his glory. He will judge the evil of abuse.

Then the LORD became jealous for his land and had pity on his people (Joel 2:18).

So the angel who talked with me said to me, 'Cry out, thus says the LORD of hosts: I am exceedingly jealous for Jerusalem and Zion' (Zechariah 1:14).

"Thus says the LORD of hosts: 'I am jealous for Zion and will dwell in the midst of Jerusalem, and Jerusalem shall be called the faithful city, and the mountain of the LORD of hosts, the holy mountain'" (Zechariah 8:2).

Full of wrath

God is wrathful against all evil and godlessness. He is furious about abuse. God will judge; justice will come.

And the LORD said to Moses, "I have seen this people, and behold, it is a stiff-necked people. Now therefore let me alone, that my wrath may burn hot against them and I may consume them, in order that I may make a great nation of you" (Exodus 32:9-10).

"Go, inquire of the LORD for me, and for the people, and for all Judah, concerning the words of this book that has been found. For great is the wrath of the LORD that is kindled against us, because our fathers have not obeyed the words of this book, to do according to all that is written concerning us." (2 Kings 22:13).

For the wrath of God is revealed from heaven against all ungodliness and unrighteousness of men, who by their unrighteousness suppress the truth (Romans 1:18).

Omnipotent

As you trust the Lord, you can trust that he is fully able to do what is consistent with his desires and character. You might have questions about God's relation to evil. This is a mystery that has troubled believers for centuries. While he is in control and powerful, people are responsible for their deeds. Studying the life of Joseph in

Scripture is helpful as we see there that while his brothers were held accountable for their sin, God was working to save lives (Genesis 50:20).

> *Who is this King of glory? The LORD, strong and mighty, the LORD, mighty in battle! (Psalm 24:8).*

> *Behold, I am the LORD, the God of all flesh. Is anything too hard for me? (Jeremiah 32:27).*

Longsuffering

There will be times when you fail and give in to fear. You can trust that the Lord is patient with you and will continue to work in your life.

> *The LORD passed before him and proclaimed, "The LORD, the LORD, a God merciful and gracious, slow to anger, and abounding in steadfast love and faithfulness" (Exodus 34:6).*

> *But you, O Lord, are a God merciful and gracious, slow to anger and abounding in steadfast love and faithfulness (Psalm 86:15).*

> *Or do you presume on the riches of his kindness and forbearance and patience, not knowing that God's kindness is meant to lead you to repentance? (Romans 2:4).*

> *What if God, desiring to show his wrath and to make known his power, has endured with much*

patience vessels of wrath prepared for destruction (Romans 9:22).

…because they formerly did not obey, when God's patience waited in the days of Noah, while the ark was being prepared, in which a few, that is, eight persons, were brought safely through water (1 Peter 3:20).

And count the patience of our Lord as salvation, just as our beloved brother Paul also wrote to you according to the wisdom given him (2 Peter 3:15).

Questions For Reflection

1. Read the attributes of God mentioned in this chapter. What does each one mean for your life?

2. In what ways have you grown in your understanding of who God is?

8. Understanding Who You Are

Impact on sense of self

Y EARS AGO, I visited someone in hospital who had been in an accident. It was common knowledge that her husband was controlling, domineering, and played mind games. While she shared about her accident, I was shocked to see that her husband, who was present, kept saying "No, that didn't happen" and then proceed to tell her what had really happened. I was even more shocked to see that she accepted his version of events as the truth (he wasn't with her when the accident occurred). During their entire marriage, she had accepted his thinking instead of her own, and came to be dependent on him for her thinking and sense of self. This can happen in parent-child relationships as well.

Breakdown in ability to think and function

If you were abused emotionally, your parent probably told you what you thought and felt, which would often contradict what you *actually* thought and felt. While growing up, you may have learned to distrust your own thoughts and come to need others to do your thinking for you, especially your parent. Accepting what your parent said they thought, saw, and experienced when it contradicted what you thought, saw, and experienced, could have led you to doubt if you can think properly for yourself.

It is important for you to learn to be responsible for your own thoughts, behavior, and for dealing with your feelings and emotions. This doesn't mean that you are to follow your heart or trust yourself, as you need a source, or authority, on which to build and test them. That authority is our life-giving Lord, whose truth is found in Scripture.

External validation

Growing up, you were probably made to understand that the way to justify your existence was to ensure that you pleased your parent. You may believe that you are, in and of yourself, unworthy.

Your parent may have raised you to do well, but only if you were not seen as better than them, and if it resulted in them receiving the credit and attention.

If you are still dependent upon your parent's thinking, you probably believe that all of your parent's frustrations, irritations, anger, shortcomings, and resentment are true – and your fault. Your sense of self is dependent on how they see you.

This could lead you to becoming dependent on external validation for your personhood. Any attempt on your part to be an individual is punished. The grievous result is that you believe that it is wrong for you to be an adult who is responsible for him or herself.

Inferior to others

You might also believe that you are inferior to other people, which can motivate you to overachieve in an attempt to feel better about yourself. You might believe that you are no good, ugly, stupid, selfish, and bad. Since your parent did not like you, and believed that you were not good enough, you might believe that you are unlikeable and inadequate. You will likely become shy, try to prove yourself to other people, and attempt to find your identity in what you do and in other people.

Loss of perspective

You may have come to hate your life and engage in self-harm to relieve the emotional pain as you believe that there is something inherently wrong with you.

Unwanted

Since you were not liked growing up, you may believe that you are damaged, and that there is something inherently wrong with you. You could have come to believe that you are unwanted and unlovable. You may desperately try to get people to love you or avoid all relationships because you believe that you will never be loved. If you do engage in relationships, you may not truly accept that the person loves you.

Scapegoat

Within the family, you could have been treated as the family scapegoat, as you were or are not as good as one of your siblings. They may be more athletic, better academically or be more physically attractive.

Who you truly are!

If you have been emotionally abused, you will have been raised to please other people, especially your parent. You existed to ensure that they felt admired and respected. Your parent is the standard for judging thoughts, behaviors, and view of self. You probably carried this into other relationships by relating to them based on what you believe they think and want. But the word of God tells us who you really are. Ephesians is a very helpful letter in this respect. By reading chapter 1, you will discover a number of life-giving truths about who you are in the Lord as a believer. Why don't you look it up?

You were chosen in Christ before the foundation of the world (1:4). Before creation you were chosen by the Lord. Your existence does not depend on your parent. The Lord willed your existence before he created the world.

Understand also that God, who created the world and all things in it (Genesis 1; Colossians 1:16), will transform your view of yourself as well. You are created in the image of God (Genesis 1:26-28), have a God-given dignity as a human being, and you reflect who God is.

You were created by and for Christ. Your existence is as valuable as everyone else's.

To be holy and blameless before him (1:4). Your purpose in life is to be holy and blameless before the Father. This purpose was given when he chose you before he created the world. Your purpose is not to please your parent, make your parent look good to other people, or give your parent satisfaction. Your focus and purpose in life is to be holy and blameless before the Father. By living this way, you will be learning to think in ways that the Lord wants. This will change how you view yourself and how you view other people. Your motive when relating to other people will change from striving to be loved and accepted (while fearing rejection), to learning to relate to them in ways that please the Lord.

Look at verse 5:

In love you were predestined for adoption through Jesus Christ, according to the purpose of his will (1:5). The Lord's motive in adopting you was love. His love is active toward you and for your good. You can live securely in the knowledge that he actively loves you and all that he does is for your good.

The choice to adopt you was made beforehand by God, according to his will. In the Greco-Roman culture, those adopted became full heirs of the family estate and were recognized as full family members. They reflected the honor of the father. Before you were a believer, you were a "child of disobedience" (2:2) and a "child of wrath" (2:3). Yet now, because of God's active love toward you, you are adopted into his family, the church!

To the praise of his glorious grace, with which he has blessed us in the Beloved (1:6). Your adoption into God's family should result in you praising him for his undeserved kindness and favor toward you. Being treated in a kind way, especially when that is not deserved, could be foreign to you. If you have lived your life trying to be loved and accepted, you might have come to believe that you cannot be loved or accepted. You might be used to being punished for failing to meet other people's expectations, being shouted at, ridiculed, ignored, slandered, or neglected. To be related to with kindness when undeserved, could be a terrifying thing for you since you have nothing in your experience to be able to understand this. While your heart's desire is to be loved, you are used to being treated in an abusive manner. Not experiencing harm, while expecting it, can be a scary place to be in.

In Christ you have the redemption through his blood, the forgiveness of your trespasses, according to the riches of his grace, which he lavished upon us, in all wisdom and insight (1:7, 8). In the Greek-speaking world, redemption referred to being delivered from prison or bondage by the payment of a sum. Redemption is seen in the Old Testament. We read about the release of slaves (Exodus 21:8; Leviticus 25:48) and Israel from slavery in Egypt (Deut 7:8; 9:26; 1 Chr 17:21). Your redemption comes through the blood of Christ, which he shed during his death on the cross. He paid the price which bought you from slavery to sin to become his property. Not only were you freed from sin at your conversion, through the work of the Holy Spirit, you continue to be freed from remaining sin and its effects on your life.

The Lord is redeeming the effects of the sin of your parent on your life. He died to purchase you, to become his possession, and to bring life. This includes bringing life into the way that you think, the way that you relate, and the heart issues you face such as anger, resentment, fear, doubt, guilt, and shame.

Having been redeemed, you have been forgiven of past, present, and future sins. Rather than holding any failure against you, the Lord forgives. You know that you have and will be forgiven because of what Christ has done on the cross. Your forgiveness does not depend on your behavior, or continuously expressing your regret. You can live in the truth that if you confess your sin, he will forgive you because he is faithful and just to do so and will cleanse you from all unrighteousness (1 John 1:9). It's not the Lord's will for you to live the rest of your life bound by the consequences of an abusive childhood. He died and rose again to redeem you, to free you from sin so that you can live a holy life to the glory of God.

The grace of God behind your redemption was lavished on you in all wisdom and insight. His grace toward you is deliberate and for your good. He is abundant in his undeserved generosity toward you. Throughout your life you may have tried in vain to be loved and accepted. In contrast, the Lord loves and accepts you when you do not deserve it. He loved and accepted you at the expense of his own Son, and continues to do so, with the purpose of your becoming holy. This holiness is for your welfare and good.

Being chosen to lead a godly and holy life makes God, and therefore Scripture, the standard or authority by which you think and live. Learning to trust your own thoughts is not the goal – the goal is that you become more holy in your thinking and so glorify God.

Being chosen, predestined for adoption, redeemed, and forgiven are all wonderful features of the truth of who you are in Christ. Being chosen by God before the foundation of the world means that you do not need external validation from your parent or any other person for your existence or who you are. But you do need an external source of truth: God himself. He chose you before the creation of the world, created you, willed your existence, predestined you for adoption, redeemed you, and forgave you. All these things are as equally true for you as for anyone else. You are not inherently inferior to other people. All people are the same before God.

Living in the truths of who God is and who you are in Christ will transform your view of yourself. As you let the Lord redeem remaining sin in your life, you will be living out of his abundant grace. When you are tempted to compare yourself to others, when you sin, or when you fail, you can know that all believers are equal in Christ and that you are certain of forgiveness because of his death on the cross. He is faithful and will forgive.

Living these truths will transform your thinking. The Lord motivates you by His Spirit and gives you purpose. Your purpose is not to win other people's love, or avoid hurt because of fear of being rejected. You can rest in the love of God, in his choosing, and his purpose. As you live in the Lord, you can learn to relate to others in loving ways that honor the Lord.

Becoming aware

For change to come, it's important that you become aware of how you think. An easy way to discover this is to keep a journal of what you think throughout the day. At the same time, you can learn to think according to what is true in Christ, such as what we just discovered in Ephesians 1. You can experience change as you examine your thoughts, and the thoughts of others, according to Scripture, and then believe and fill your mind with biblical truth.

There may be certain things that you do when you are more inclined to dwell on what others have said about you and how they have treated you. Your thoughts will probably progress to believing what they say. If you discover *when* you tend to do this, you can be watchful and stop such thoughts and focus on what is true. It could be helpful for you to have biblical truths hanging in places where you are tempted to think negatively. I know people who have stuck notes with Bible verses on them above the kitchen sink and next to the cooker. They have also written verses on cards or on their phone when going to visit their family. You can also listen to podcasts and music to help you focus on helpful things, speak Scripture out loud, or even sing.

Laura's story

While Laura was growing up, her mother would tell her what she (Laura) was thinking and feeling. She was told if she was tired or sick, even when she felt fine. Her mother would give her the reasons why she behaved in certain ways, even though the reasons given were not what Laura actually thought. But since it was her mother, Laura thought she must be right as she knew better. She started checking with her mother to know what to think and how to behave in certain situations.

Being dependent on her mother meant that she believed that she had to make sure that her mother was happy and not angry or upset. If she was angry or lonely, Laura was to blame and had to fix it. She often wondered what it was about her brother Mark that caused him to receive mother's praise and affection. Her mother would talk to Mark about how much better he was than Laura and expressed her frustration to Laura that she couldn't be more like her brother.

Laura started to write down what she was thinking throughout the day. She considered whether what she believed was true according to what the Bible says about her. She memorized what the Lord had done for her and who she is in him from Ephesians chapter 1. She would take what she found she habitually thought and then compare it to that chapter. To help her after being with people who she was intimidated by, she would place those truths around her house where she was inclined to think negatively and dwell on what they said and did.

Questions For Reflection

1.   What have you believed about who you really are?

2.   Read Ephesians chapter 1. Who are you in Christ?

9. Other Reactions and How To Deal With Them

Depression

BELIEVING THAT YOU must obtain love and approval, but never being able to, could lead to depression. This is especially the case if you believe that you are a failure, unlovable, unwanted, and that there is something wrong with you. This can be compounded when these things are said to you, when you are compared negatively to a sibling, and are told that you have no right to exist. As an adult, this might continue when others judge you and put you down.

When you feel depressed, you will probably believe that you are not able to take up your responsibilities or accomplish things, resulting in feeling even more depressed, and it can lead to suicidal thoughts or attempts.

Helpful steps include:

- Work on your thinking patterns
- Keeping a schedule
- Taking regular physical exercise

- Having social contact
- Having set times for going to bed and getting up in the morning
- Developing healthy eating patterns

Start by doing one responsible thing every day, and then develop this over a period of time so that you are keeping a weekly schedule.

Write down the things that you will think about when you are inclined to think sad thoughts. Focus on Christ, who he is, what he has done, and who you are in him. Your hope is found in him. He is the one who gives you purpose and who defines who you are; it is not based on what others say or have said about you.

Guilt and shame

Having grown up in a home where you were constantly criticized, blamed, mocked, and held to an impossibly high standard of behavior, you will probably live in a state of guilt and shame. Memories of times when your parent mocked and shamed you might come back intrusively.

You could believe that things are your fault and therefore live in a state of guilt. You may continue to think that it is your fault that you were treated that way. It is *your* fault that your parent made the choices that they did, experienced the feelings that they had, and behaved in the way that they did. It is your fault that your parent did not love you.

Believing that there is something inherently wrong

with you that caused this to happen means that you live in a state of shame. You believe that you are bad, selfish, that there is something wrong with you, and that you are damaged.

It will help you to think through what your God-given responsibilities are. These include your thoughts, your motives, your behavior, your work, and your time. Write these out and think through how Scripture addresses each one and what it means to honor the Lord in each. Then list your parent's and other people's responsibilities. This includes their thoughts, dealing with their motives, behaviors, work, and use of their time.

Next, list *your* concerns. These include all other things in life which are not responsibilities; for example, what other people think of you, and other people's emotions. If you accept other people's responsibilities as your own, or your everyday concerns become things that you are responsible for, you will not have the means to be able to do them. Since you do not have the means to be responsible for these things, taking them as *responsibilities* in your life will lead to anger, frustration, anxiety, and disappointment.

You will probably struggle with guilt if you have responded to the abuse by becoming addicted to a substance to relieve your emotional pain, or if you have responded by becoming critical, angry toward others, or self-protective. It's crucial that you know that the abuse was not your fault. The answer to guilt is understanding what Christ did on the cross.

When we look at what Christ did on the cross, we know that God cares for our suffering. This includes *your* suffering. Jesus became sin for you so that you might become righteous.

> *For our sake he made him to be sin who knew no sin, so that in him we might become the righteousness of God (2 Corinthians 5:21).*

In other words, those who have placed their faith in Christ are imputed with his righteousness.

Romans chapter 5 includes the statement:

> *For as by the one man's disobedience the many were made sinners, so by the one man's obedience the many will be made righteous (Romans 5:19).*

Believers have been credited with his perfect righteousness. Paul teaches us that believers are justified by the grace of God as a gift, through the redemption that is in Christ. Jesus was a propitiation by His blood. In other words, this means that God's wrath has been turned away from the sinner by the sacrifice of Jesus Christ on the cross.

> *…and are justified by his grace as a gift, through the redemption that is in Christ Jesus, whom God put forward as a propitiation by his blood, to be received by faith. This was to show God's righteousness, because in his divine forbearance [his patience] he had passed over former sins (Romans 3:24-25 – my insert).*

God's wrath is toward sin and anything that is opposed to his character, which humanly speaking we deserve. Christ bore this wrath by being that propitiation. In Romans 5:6-11, we also learn that Jesus was our substitute.

> *For while we were still weak, at the right time Christ died for the ungodly. For one will scarcely die for a righteous person—though perhaps for a good person one would dare even to die— but God shows his love for us in that while we were still sinners, Christ died for us. Since, therefore, we have now been justified by his blood, much more shall we be saved by him from the wrath of God. For if while we were enemies we were reconciled to God by the death of his Son, much more, now that we are reconciled, shall we be saved by his life. More than that, we also rejoice in God through our Lord Jesus Christ, through whom we have now received reconciliation.*

Jesus took our place by bearing the wrath of God for us, resulting in us being reconciled to God. In Colossians 1:22 we discover that being reconciled to God, we are holy, blameless, and above reproach.

He has now reconciled you to God by his death on the cross, in order to present you holy and blameless and above reproach before him. Your hope, if you feel guilty and shameful, is found in Christ and what he has done on the cross.

The key to this is your understanding of justification.

Since you are a believer who has repented of your sin and trusted Christ for forgiveness, recognizing that he took your place when he paid your punishment on the cross, you can know that you have been forgiven of all guilt. This forgiveness depends on the completed work of Christ on the cross, not on how you, or other people, think about you.

You are standing in a position of righteousness before God because of what Christ did on the cross. This is who you truly are. You can live in this truth by bringing each condemning thought about yourself and replacing it with the truth that you are declared righteous. You must saturate your thinking with this truth, especially at times when you are tempted to think otherwise.

Shame

We first see shame in the Bible in Genesis 3:7, when Adam and Eve covered themselves because they were naked. This is in contrast to Genesis 2:25, when Adam and Eve experienced no shame about being naked during the period of innocence before the Fall in chapter 3. The human experience of shame is a result of the guilt of sinning against God. The shame of nakedness is seen again in 2 Samuel chapter 10, when a king called Hanun shamed David's men by stripping them of their clothes and shaving off half of each man's beard. In that cultural context, the shame experienced was a result of a deliberate attempt by Hanun's men to humiliate David's men.

In the gospel, we see that Jesus associated with those who were shamed by others because they were seen to be inferior. Examples are the woman at the well (John 4:1-45) and tax collectors and sinners (Matthew 9:9-13).

By dying on the cross, Jesus died in a shameful way, being naked and exposed to everybody who was looking at him. He fulfilled the prophecy in Isaiah chapter 53:3-5, knowing the shame of being "as one from whom men hide their faces, he was despised, and we esteemed him not." Even though he was innocent, he suffered shame so that others would be made righteous. Through his death and resurrection, Jesus canceled the debt that is against you (Colossians 2:14). As a result, as a believer, you have become the righteousness of God (2 Corinthians 5:21). You have been justified by faith through Christ (Romans 5:1). There is now no condemnation for you (Romans 8:1). You are to live according to God's plan for you: being holy and blameless before him (Ephesians 1:4).

You are righteous in Christ because of his work on the cross. Your shame has been borne by him, so that you can now live a godly life. Your alienation from God has been removed by Christ so that you may be holy and blameless before him (Colossians 1:21, 22).

So instead of accepting your parent's judgment of you, you can learn to see yourself as Jesus does. By nature, you are a sinner who does not match God's perfect standard and is cut off from God. But as a believer, you have been clothed with the righteousness of Christ because of his work on the cross. You belong to Christ, even if your parent rejects and excludes you. You can know that Christ has removed your shame in a personal and intimate way. In Isaiah 54:4-6 it says that the LORD comforts Israel by saying that she is to forget her shame, as he, her Maker, is her husband. This is true of the church, the bride of Christ (Revelation 21:1-4). As a believer, you are part of the bride of Christ. You are to live out of the truth that, in him, you are holy and without blemish (Ephesians 5:27).

Anger

You might experience times of being hostile and angry, as result of being frustrated, punished, blamed, and held back. You might become angry when you realize that you should have experienced love from the person who was responsible for you and should have cared for you and protected you. You may experience anger at the depth of the selfishness of your parent.

Anger, by nature, comes from a judgment that you are against something and perceive it to be wrong. An angry person will have imaginary conversations in which they are paying the person back or are silencing someone with a brilliantly placed last word. Anger can lead to fighting and arguing with others, holding grudges, planning revenge, slandering other people, and causing factions. You might have become bitter because of the way you've been treated and want to, or have acted on that anger, i.e. taken some form of revenge.

While it is right to be angry about the evil of abuse, it is crucial to have a biblical view about your anger. Anger is more than an emotion. When we are mad, our whole person judges something to be wrong. It's right for our entire person to judge abuse as being evil.

But for our anger to be righteous, it must include the following:

1. A sin that has occurred.
2. A concern for the glory of God and not our own glory.
3. A righteous expression of that anger.

Abuse is a sin and is opposed to the nature of who God is. Due to this, it is right to be angry. However, it is important to let the Lord work on your heart so that your anger does not become sinful. To do this, you can examine your heart when you are angry. You could ask yourself questions such as, "What did I say and do when I became angry?", "What did I say to myself when I became angry?" and "What did I want from other people?" It's important to remember that justice will prevail. The abuser will not "get away with it."

Numbness

You might have cut yourself off from your situation as a way of coping while you were growing up. This means you are emotionally numb and have shut down your emotions. You might feel nothing, let your mind go blank, and stare off into space. Please read or listen to the section in chapter 4 about disengaged thinking for when you are tempted to respond in this way.

Grief

When you see the true nature of your parent, you could experience grief and mourn what was done to you.

Yet your hope is in Christ, the 'man of sorrows' who bore *your* sorrows.

> *He was despised and rejected by men, a man of sorrows and acquainted with grief; and as one from whom men hide their faces he was despised, and we esteemed him not (Isaiah 53:3).*

Loneliness

You might feel that you do not belong anywhere. Loneliness is an emotionally painful sense of not being connected to others. A lonely person may feel alone, unwanted, isolated, and left out. It can be the result of living in fear, being isolated from others, a lack of intimacy with God, a lack of emotional connection with others, and a sense of being rejected by your parent.

Questions For Reflection

1. What do you think about when you feel sad? What is true of you in Christ?

2. List your responsibilities and concerns and the responsibilities of others. When have you taken other people's responsibilities as your own?

3. When you are angry, what do you want from other people? What do you think, say, and do when you are angry?

10. The Reality of Evil and the Victory in Christ

THE EVIL INTENTIONS and suffering involved in abuse are a result of living in a fallen world. After Adam and Eve rebelled against God's commands in Genesis 3, sin and suffering entered creation. Before their rebellion, as we see in Genesis 1 and 2, there was no suffering, pain, or sin. Creation was declared to be "good", and Adam and Eve "very good". They lived their purpose of reflecting the character of God by being his image-bearers in creation. It was after they chose to disobey God, which we read about in Genesis 3, that they experienced suffering, death, relational problems, sin, fear, and shame. These disastrous effects were also seen in their son, Cain, who murdered his innocent brother, Abel, because of anger and jealousy

> Now Adam knew Eve his wife, and she conceived and bore Cain, saying, "I have gotten a man with the help of the LORD." And again, she bore his brother Abel. Now Abel was a keeper of sheep, and Cain a worker of the ground. In the course of time Cain brought to the LORD an offering of the fruit of the ground, and Abel also brought of the

firstborn of his flock and of their fat portions. And the LORD had regard for Abel and his offering, but for Cain and his offering he had no regard…

Cain spoke to Abel his brother. And when they were in the field, Cain rose up against his brother Abel and killed him (Genesis 4:1-8).

Abel was a worshipper of the Lord who had done no wrong toward Cain. Yet he suffered innocently at the hands of his brother. The disastrous consequences continued as Lamech later killed a man.

The story continues in Genesis 4.

Lamech said to his wives: "Adah and Zillah, hear my voice; you wives of Lamech, listen to what I say: I have killed a man for wounding me, a young man for striking me. If Cain's revenge is sevenfold, then Lamech's is seventy-sevenfold." (Genesis 4:23, 24).

We too live in a world that is fallen, is cursed, is full of suffering, where people commit evil against others.

Evil conquered

But evil does not reign and does not have the final say. Through his death on the cross, Jesus defeated Satan and evil. It was at the cross that Christ disarmed the rulers and authorities, putting them to open shame, and triumphing over them.

He disarmed the rulers and authorities and put

them to open shame, by triumphing over them in him (Colossians 2:15).

Jesus has fulfilled Psalm 110:1 as he is seated at the right hand of the Father in heaven, having defeated God's enemies.

The LORD says to my Lord: "Sit at my right hand, until I make your enemies your footstool."

That power is the same as the mighty strength he worked in Christ when he raised him from the dead and seated him at his right hand in the heavenly places, far above all rule and authority and power and dominion, and above every name that is named, not only in this age but also in the one to come (Ephesians 1:19-21).

We read elsewhere that he destroyed the devil and that the reason why the Son of God appeared was to destroy his works.

Since therefore the children share in flesh and blood, he himself likewise partook of the same things, that through death he might destroy the one who has the power of death, that is, the devil (Hebrews 2:14).

Whoever makes a practice of sinning is of the devil, for the devil has been sinning from the beginning. The reason the Son of God appeared was to destroy the works of the devil (1 John 3:8).

Even at the worst moment in history, when Adam

and Eve had chosen to rebel against God, he graciously promised that evil would be conquered. He announced that the seed of the woman would bruise the serpent's head, i.e. the seed of the woman would bruise the devil.

> *I will put enmity between you and the woman, and between your offspring and her offspring; he shall bruise your head, and you shall bruise his heel." (Genesis 3:15.*

Through his victory on the cross, Christ has transferred believers from the domain of darkness to the kingdom of his Son where there is the forgiveness of sins.

> *He has delivered us from the domain of darkness and transferred us to the kingdom of his beloved Son, in whom we have redemption, the forgiveness of sins (Colossians 1:13, 14).*

Sin conquered

Jesus suffered in the place of sinners, substituting himself for them on the cross. He fulfilled the righteous requirements of the law, thereby satisfying the justice of God in the place of sinners.

The guilt, which must be punished because of God's just nature, is covered, or satisfied, by the death of Christ on the cross. The result is that the sinner is pardoned. Christ was made a curse for us by bearing our sins on the cross. Because our punishment was placed on him, if a person trusts in Christ and what he accomplished on the cross, he or she can be forgiven and come into a new relationship with God.

> *Christ redeemed us from the curse of the law by becoming a curse for us—for it is written, "Cursed is everyone who is hanged on a tree" (Galatians 3:13).*

Satan and death conquered

After promising that the seed of the woman would crush the serpent's head, the Son of God later became human. He destroyed the devil who had the power of death and delivered those who through fear of death were subject to lifelong slavery.

> *…that through death he might destroy the one who has the power of death, that is, the devil, and deliver all those who through fear of death were subject to lifelong slavery (Hebrews 2:14b-15).*

You know that evil is real. It's possible that at times you wondered if evil is more powerful than God. Thankfully, evil has been defeated by Jesus at the cross, as have the devil and his works. The Lord has paid for the evil of abuse. It will not have the final say. Jesus' work on the cross is more extensive than his glorious conquering of sin: he also defeated evil, Satan and his works, and death. You can trust God that he is just, and that evil will be punished.

Laura's story

Laura could see the effects of her mother in her emotional reactions as an adult. At times she would be angry at missing out on the unconditional mother-love that most people experience. At other times, she would become numb. This was especially true on Mother's Day and at Christmas. As Laura listened to teaching at her church about the Lord Jesus and what he has done, she came to a deeper understanding of the cross. He paid for all of her guilt and shame and clothed her with his righteousness. As she learned about the attributes of God, her understanding of him deepened, and this helped her, especially when she was inclined to worry.

This was also true regarding her self-protectiveness in relationships, particularly when she became anxious about how they would respond to her, or when she was being faced with having to trust people. She learned to relate to people in ways that would encourage and bless them.

Questions For Reflection

1. What has been conquered at the cross?

2. What does this mean for the abuse you have suffered?

Closing Thoughts

PARENTS CAN BE vindictive and cruel to their children. Not all parents protect their children. We've seen how abusive parents can treat their children and how this impacts their behavior, sense of self, thinking, relating, and emotions. But in Christ, you have hope. As you trust and learn from him the Lord will restore you in each of these areas.

In the many years the Lord has given me to serve those who have suffered abuse, I have seen him transform and change hundreds of people. He has begun a wonderful work in your life, changing you to become more like him. You can live a life defined by Christ!

Bibliography

Berger, Daniel. *Mental Illness: The Influence of Nurture. Volume Four.* Taylors: Alethia Publications, 2016.

Berkhof, Louis. *Systematic Theology.* Carlisle: Banner of Truth, 1996.

Berkouwer, G.C. *Studies in Dogmatics: Sin.* Grand Rapids: Eerdmans Publishing, 1980.

Cori, Jasmin Lee. *The Emotionally Absent Mother: How to Recognize and Heal the Invisible Effects of Childhood Emotional Neglect.* New York: The Experiment, 2017.

Dryburgh, Anne. *Debilitated & Diminished: Help for Christian Women in Emotionally Abusive Marriages,* Create Space, 2018.

_____. *(Un)Ashamed: Christ's Transforming Hope for Rape Victims.* Kansas City: Pure Water Press, 2020.

Farmer, Steven. *Adult Children of Abusive Parents: A Healing Program for those who have Been Physically, Sexually, or Emotionally Abused.* Fort Wayne: Earth Magic Books, 2015.

Forward, Susan. *Mothers Who Can't Love: A Healing Guide for Daughters.* New York: HarperCollins, 2013.

Golomb, Elan. *Trapped in the Mirror: Adult Children of Narcissists in their Struggle for Self.* New York: William Morrow and Company Inc, 1992.

Grossman, Frances, Joseph Spinazzola, Marla Zucker, & Elizabeth Hopper. *Treating Adult Survivors of Childhood Emotional Abuse & Neglect: A New Framework.* American Journal of Orthopsychiatry, 2017, Vol. 87, No. 1, 86-93.

Grudem, Wayne. *Systematic Theology: An Introduction to Systematic Theology.* Grand Rapids: Zondervan Publishing, 1994.

Herman, Judith. *Trauma and Recovery: The Aftermath of Violence – From Domestic Abuse to Political Terror.* New York: Basic Books, 2015.

_____. "Complex PTSD: A Syndrome in Survivors of Prolonged and Repeated Trauma." *Journal of Traumatic Stress* Vol. 5. No. 3, 1992.

Hopper, Elizabeth, Frances Grossman, Joseph Spinazzola & Marla Zucker. *Treating Adult Survivors of Childhood Emotional Abuse and Neglect: Component-Based Psychotherapy.* New York: The Guilford Press, 2019.

Horwitz, Allan, Cathy Widom, Julie McLaughlin, Helene White. "The Impact of Childhood Abuse and

Neglect on Adult Mental Health: A Prospective Study." *Journal of Health and Social Behavior* Jun 2001 42:2.

Lambert, Heath. *A Theology of Biblical Counseling: The Doctrinal Foundations of Counseling Ministry.* Grand Rapids: Zondervan Publishing, 2016.

Lanius, Ruth, Eric Vermettern, Claire Pain. *The Impact of Early Life Trauma on Health and Disease: The Hidden Epidemic.* Cambridge: Cambridge University Press, 2010.

Longman, Tremper III & David Garland. *The Expositor's Bible Commentary 12: Ephesians – Philemon.* Grand Rapids: Zondervan Academic, 2006.

MacMillan Harriet. "Childhood Abuse and Lifetime Psychopathology in a Community Sample." *Am J Psychiatry* 158:11 November 2001.

McBride, Karyl. *Will I Ever be Good Enough: Healing the Daughters of Narcissistic Mothers.* New York: Atria Paperback, 2008.

Macey, Diana. *Narcissistic Mothers and Covert Emotional Abuse.* Independently Published, 2017.

Merkle, Benjamin. *ESV Expository Commentary: Ephesians.* Wheaton: Crossway, 2018.

Morrigan, Danu. *You're Not Crazy – It's Your Mother.* London: Darton, Longman, and Todd Ltd, 2012.

Powlison, David. *Safe & Sound: Standing Firm in Spiritual Battles,* Greensboro: New Growth Press, 2019.

Rice, Linda. *Parenting the Difficult Child: A Biblical Perspective on Reactive Attachment Disorder.* Seedsown Press, 2012.

Smith, David. *With Willful Intent: A Theology of Sin.* Eugene: Wipf and Stock Publishers, 2003.

Tracy. Stephen. *Mending the Soul: Understanding and Healing Abuse.* Grand Rapids: Zondervan, 2005.

Venning, Ralph. *The Sinfulness of Sin.* Carlisle: Banner of Truth Trust, 1965.

CPSIA information can be obtained
at www.ICGtesting.com
Printed in the USA
LVHW080819200222
711543LV00022B/2593